FRENCH FOR SOLDIERS

Also by Nina Nyhart:
OPENERS

FRENCH FOR SOLDIERS

·|·   ·|·   ·|·

poems by

NINA NYHART

Alice James Books
Cambridge, Massachusetts

Cover and book design by Colleen McCallion
Typography by Arlington Graphics, Inc.

Library of Congress Catalogue Card Number 86-72478
ISBN 0-914086-70-7 (cloth)
ISBN 0-914086-71-5 (paper)

Grateful acknowledgment is made to the editors of the
following publications in which some of these poems first
appeared: *The Nantucket Review, Newton Free Library
Anthology, Ploughshares, Puckerbrush Review, The Radcliffe
Quarterly, Shenandoah, Sojourner, The Worcester Review,
Zeugma.* "Tennis" was reprinted in *Anthology of Magazine
Verse & Yearbook of American Poetry, 1981.*

My gratitude to The MacDowell Colony where some of
these poems were written.

The publication of this book was made possible with support
from the National Endowment for the Arts, Washington,
D.C., and from the Massachusetts Council on the Arts &
Humanities, a state agency whose funds are recommended
by the Governor and appropriated by the State Legislature.

Alice James Books are published by the Alice James
Poetry Cooperative, Inc.

Alice James Books
138 Mount Auburn Street
Cambridge, Massachusetts 02138

for my mother and father

CONTENTS

I

II

III

IV

FRENCH FOR SOLDIERS: A Language Lesson

Where are we   We are in the trenches
Where are they   They are in the shelter
Have you any tools   No, I haven't any
What do you have   I have a string

                    bucket   helmet
                    screwdriver   overcoat
                    coffee   stew
                    water   mud

The Englishmen are tall
The Frenchwomen are pretty
The Belgians are poor
The Germans are in the steeple

Where is the church   It is behind the trees
Have they any cannon   They have a great many
We have no spades   Who has the axe

The Americans are in the town
We give the bread to the Belgians
Ten Germans are in the window of the steeple

                    Hands up!   Halt!
                    Get up!   Surrender!
                    Where are your dugouts
                    Where is the command post
                    How many machine guns have you

I got up this morning
You washed your face
He shaved himself
They have cut the buttons off
   the trousers of the German

The attack of the enemy is going to fail
We will riddle them with bullets
When will we be in England

> the first of January
> the second of January
> next month
> in spring
> in summer
> in autumn

Then from one thing to another, M. Hamel began to speak to us of the French language, saying that it was the most beautiful language in the world, the most clear, the most solid:

> I am
> thou art
> he is
> we are
> you are
> they are

that it was necessary to keep it among us and never forget it, because, when a people falls into slavery, as long as it keeps its language, it is as if it held the key of its prison.

gun   butt
breech   trigger
sight   barrel
tripod   ejector

Then he took a grammar and read us our lesson.

We had to go
It was necessary to go
We must go
We shall have to go

I was astonished to see how I understood. All that he said seemed to me easy, easy.

flame projector
bomb thrower
heavy batteries
explosive charge

I think also that I had never listened so well, and that he also had never put so much patience into his explanations.

to call the roll
to fill up the gaps
to carry off the wounded
to bury the dead

*One would have said that before going away the poor man wished
to give us all his knowledge, to make it enter our heads with a
single stroke.*

They made us retreat
He is going to make us advance
Put on your respirators
Here is a gas cloud
Lie down
Get up

> *Come children of the fatherland*
> *The glorious day has come*
> *To arms, citizens*
> *Let us march, march*
> *Let a foul blood*
> *Drench our furrows*

Where are the wounded
Where is the dressing station
Have you seen the ambulance
Do you feel much pain

That hurts me
I am feverish
Where are we
You are in France

·|·

Adapted from *French For Soldiers*, Harvard University Press, 1917.
Italicized passages are from Alphonse Daudet's story "The
Last Lesson" and from "The Marseillaise."

THREE MAGRITTES

CECI N'EST PAS UNE POMME

This is not an apple.
And it's not "not an apple"
but looks precisely like an apple
—stem and four green leaves—

a sign that once a tooth
pierces the skin, the river will rise,
overflow its banks,
and the red swimmer will leap onto the tongue.

When the leaves grow a little stiff...
when the stem darkens...
when the apple tips to light...

but *ceci n'est pas une pomme,* this is canvas
and paint and the eye of the painter—
window orchard stone and tree—

no, not an orchard. This is a mind,
round and shining, with a green bird
perched on it,
a bird with celestial penmanship.

LE THÉRAPEUTE

The therapist wears a hat
but no head.

Stone cape, stone legs and shoes,
he casts a shadow though

"real" isn't the word for the one
who looks at you without eyes.

Looking for him is like looking for
your glasses—how can you see to see?

Left hand on a sack of keepsakes,
right hand on a cane,
he must have stopped to rest.

Something moves—
a child wants to speak...

He waits by the sea,
a silence with a gate in it

and two fat gatekeepers
with calm and folded wings.

L'USAGE DE LA PAROLE

The stars spell out *D É S I R*
and what's a word for
if not to hang in shining pieces
in a midnight sky?

Lakes of ink on the grass,
inky trees, houses,

and inside—a dreamer,
a specialist in turning speech
to wheels of fire.

When the cobalt air strikes her lips
she sends up the alphabet.

But as the great shadow crosses borders
and midnight keeps happening,
will the dreamer travel too—
her lexicon expand galactically?

What signs, then, will she whisper
into light?

TURNSTILE

I wasn't exactly born, more like thrown
from a train whistling through the bright
Pennsylvania fields. I held a pencil
in my hand & I was taking notes. I wrote
dirt & scarecrow & blackwing shadows...
I remember large disinterested persons speaking
while sprouts pushed up through hard ground
& then I wrote a regular bill of rights:
vegetable, animal, mineral, personal.

I strode through the humming grass writing
my feet rearrange the lives of thousands.
It must have been summer moving into fall
when I recorded this remarkable program:
The Seasons, & though I expected rain
& briars, I came instead to a turnstile.
Sure there was another field, sure sky,
but no one to say how to go through, or why.

Muscles would be needed, lungpower,
& for all I knew—hooves or claws.
It was growing cold, the days shorter,
my notes longer. I wrote *who am I without*
this first field, these first words?
But that was history. The stile beckoned,
I tucked my pencil behind my ear, opened
my eyes & spun on through, primed for crossings
unimagined, unimaginable, from the train.

THE HIGHWAYMAN

I don't know if the moon is full or what,
and I'm not getting up to look or
check the click of the motion detector,
but a second ago I picked up the sound of a tape—
chatter stretched flat as a ribbon
or an old road lit by moonlight...

A woman read to me.

She'd look up, knowing the words to come,
not seeing how scared I was—
she in a chair in my room holding a book—
me lying in bed caught in some grippe.
I bought the whole package: sickness, poem, mother,
and that whacko highwayman,
the one I knew would gallop his bright black horse
under the next full moon
right up that ribbon of light, knock on the old inn door
and ask for me.

I'd have to answer.

Mother wouldn't be there—she'd be enjoying her voice.
The choice was mine: there wasn't any:
I'd do whatever he said.
Then she'd say It's time for sleep.
But it wasn't sleep he came for.
It was the real thing
and nothing could stop him or his clippetyclop
or the knock or that shiny black ribbon of voice, oh yes.

HOME

"You can't get there from here," they said,
they said *can't,* so I ran for the plane

that landed on my childhood lane turned
turnpike: vapor lights, Wrong Way, the works.

Aluminum boxes, asbestos roofs sprayed
up the hill like shrapnel. On top—

two glass giants—Bonwit's, Saks.
Nowhere a scruffy road, no red barn or house.

"You'll never find it," they said *never,*
so I put on a hardhat, constructed some country:

pastures, fences, thriving oaks. Deep
in those green velvet circles, acres of woods,

I placed a stream and stones,
a pond to shelter tadpoles, handle thirst.

UNIVERSITY

I didn't know what was in it for me,
creeping past eternity, the classics,
et cetera. Still, what better place
to clinch a deal, atmosphere so thin
I could leave the floor, replace

the birds, and really think.
I knew birds—Heidegger, Kant—gentle
flutterers cluttering the beige ionosphere.
Traipsing marble halls I thought
proposals he might like, or fight,

when we came to the green baize table.
Tomorrow: the parley, this interperson
bingo-bang. A voice warned "Look you cubs
get up those trees, this real good
school don't tolerate no sloppy."

I wore my mac, galoshes, it didn't rain,
but stomach-crash and worse below.
I'd brought the quill, onionskin, wax
and matches, but suddenly my plan lacked
starch. I grabbed the Louis-something chair,

sat tall, blabbed "I want true
education!" Birds were building
a lapse of words right there in my throat.
Had I gone too far? The room swirled.
He took my hand, touched everything, signed.

TENNIS

In the hotel room, on tour,
before the match,
boy bringing bad coffee, burnt toast,

I answer the phone: my opponent.
Peaches and champagne I say,
winding up, serving breakfast.

If only I could jump the net, shake hands,
retire, design a line of sportswear,
redesign the sport: no judge or score,

no spin or slice or smash.
No cash. Green would be green
and white the light the players dance

within. *And croissants flown in*
this morning, I add, as if winning
were flying, as if I loved games.

THE WHOLE STORY

It was a beautiful day at the beach,
cobalt sky winging down to meet the silver sea.
Wind roared toward the south, but two rogue hulls

had fled their moorings, barreled due north.
I wanted to make a move as lovely as those many-
colored Cariocans ambling their sugary shore.

Feeling opulent, I endowed a chair, a table,
a whole condo for a dark professor,
smack on dunes—guaranteed to slide one day

into surf—but right then fixed to the view.
The next minute a newborn washed up on the sand,
speaking through a set of thirty-two shiny teeth.

How could I tell what would come of this—
the stunning day, the beach's negritude,
good will surging and that sharklet just landed

for a leap-month of molars, incisors, bicuspids.
How to fathom the message in the babble—
something big and bad, but also gone and dead.

Was this the past? Should I be afraid? What hidden
currents sped those rogue hulls? The truth
seemed dappled, elusive as that shadowy teacher

I was preparing for. The one who'd hear
the whole story for what I wanted it to be—
generous, integrated, salty, and with teeth.

IN A DREAM OF ABE LINCOLN, A VOICE SAYS
You don't get pleasure from the truth.

So.
   It's lies stroke the belly till it curls,
lies that stack up like Lincoln Logs,
   a sturdy house in the wilderness.

Praise the pack of lies that roams the Illinois
   riverbank. Praise the fisherman's giant lie
and the small fish for its pain.
   Praise fish for brainfood which is a lie.

Praise brain that tells body when to rise
   and when to lie by the fire and dream.
Praise a poem that floats downstream
   tipping its tall black hat.

DREAM CURE

Because in his new life he's a palomino,
he wants to show me how he sleeps
with his wife—gold flanks against white sheets,
manes spread on pillows, nostrils opening, closing—
while I stand there, embarrassed,
counting *hoof hoof hoof hoof hoof*...

And now he's alone, still in bed—sick—
rattles in the ribcage—
and I've the surefire cure:
The Chinese Breakfast Tray.
First I prepare the room—exotic,
but not mandarin. This takes about thirty

seconds. Tea water is boiling
and I'm cutting up the delicious
rice paper for him, pleased at how well
everything is progressing.
He has confidence in me, too,
which is the real cure, we both know,

but fail to mention for reasons of diplomacy.
The tray must be made of bamboo,
with strong legs, and must be placed
at precisely the correct angle to his chest.
This cure has worked for centuries in my family,
and I can see it's working now for him

as he leans back on the pillow
and spreads his arms wrapped in the red and blue
stripes of a boy's soccer sleeves,
his cheeks glistening after play,
generations of excellent health
roaring through him.

THE SHOES

You can't just go into the shoe store and say
"I want those maroon shoes"—so you stop
at the cleaners. Waiting at the counter
you spot the two red maple leaves.
You're wondering what wayward tree dropped them
when Mrs. Tony slips them into your lapel.
It's a radiant fall day like
                                    the ones years ago
when you worried about falling, what with one leg
shorter, the foot smaller. That's how you learned
about balance, imbalance, and how on a horse,
English saddle, the stirrups never hung right because
who could explain to a riding instructor, in English,
a thing so difficult, so private.
                                    It's October now,
leaves settle down to be kicked as in the old days,
but your left foot refused to do that, being
damaged itself. Meanwhile your right foot
was growing up correctly rushing out to give
a shove to any leaf or pebble foolish enough
to lie in its path.
                        So when Mrs. Tony leans
across the counter to award the two red medals,
you notice the leaves aren't alike—one scarred,
the other larger. You both smile. You pivot,
head for the door and the store where you saw
those maroon shoes, in the window, glowing,
perfectly mismatched.

II

JACK LOOKS BACK

Always achieving—never a chief. I tried, God knows.
Out of the box, over the candle, up the hill—I ran
like hell. I swear Jill tripped me. My head
still throbs. I took lessons from magicians, quick-
change artists, apes, asses, hares,
even listened to a small green preacher in the woods.

I was one busy boy, but didn't know beans—would
sell a cow for some. When I put them up my nose
Ma made a fuss. Women! I'd like a harem,
but *one*—forget it. After that I ran
up the beanstalk, zapped the old bloke & quick
as a wink—split. They called me headstrong,

foolhardy, but I made headway—
you develop a sense... Besides, it wouldn't
do to leave the women unprotected. Quick
with a knife, I had a strong arm & a nose
for giants. I wore my magic cap, ran
like blazes, came within a hair's

breadth of being ground to powder. A hairy
adolescence. One fell headlong
into my camouflaged pit—that was Cormoran.
Blunderbore was worse. He axed the bundled wood
in my bed instead of me & paid through the nose—
kaput. You've got to kill quick,

brother, to stay quick.
Now I dress like the others, wear my hair
neat, keep lean & work with a weather nose
for news. When it turns cold I slip in, just ahead
of winter. I've tried lumbering, but woods
try me. I miss the gray alleys that ran

like shadows through the city, the guys I ran
with as a kid. You learned quickly
in the city, or any old giant would
rip you off, or woman. Sometimes my hair
stood on end when those beautiful heads
rolled. Now I search old haunts, pub-crawl. Who knows

who I'll find. Last night I ran across a girl—red hair
to her waist. Quick! I thought—head
home. Keep your nose clean. Deep breath. Knock wood.

THE FILMMAKER

You wake full of celluloid and plots—
a war vet murders his kids... lots

of yellows—a wheatfield, a blond mother.
And three little boys—your brothers.

That's when you remember your old man
drinking mash, yelling, grabbing his gun...

You raced for the barn, slid under. Chest
pounding manure, you held your breath—

> *I know where you are   Come outa
> there brats or I'll hafta shoot*

Now you head for the set, the scene zinging
in your skull, the yellowjacket sting

of a truelife story. You're ready to cast
when a woman wearing white socks runs past

shrieking *Arthur! Don't do it!* Air
leaves your lungs at last. Ma's there.

You reach for the camera, aim low,
shoot as silently as you know how.

THE FILMMAKER'S GIRLFRIEND

He's making a film about screaming,
a shower, a slow-motion murder
(which you deserve because
no one has ever done anything
as terrible as you have).

He shoots it over and over
as if he can't get it right.
He gets it right.
He wants to hear that perfect scream
once more. It's how he knows he scores.

The film ends but the nightmare
goes on—copies flood movie houses,
bulbs flash, fame stalks your body
smeared on mags, posters, pillows.
Everyone wants a piece of the actress.

He wants, he says, the money.
You want to sleep again—
without dreams—
without that red-streaked water
swirling down the drain.

You want the plot where
he drops you for the script-girl.
She hangs bigger, drowns deeper,
shrieks higher.
Let her be discovered.
Let him show her how to live forever.

MATCH GIRL

It isn't the cold that gets to her,
though her fingers are stones
in the dark. Nor the dark, hiding

its thieves. It's looking into
a yellow room, seeing mouths move,
children dart like tropical birds.

It's watching a family curve around
an oak table, eating bread, peeling
oranges. Fastened to the silent side

of the glass, she clings nameless
as a moth, or an orphan in a fairy tale
who freezes to death gracefully,

entering a vision of homecoming,
an aura of golden light.
That's when she takes a deep breath,

grabs the trash, the oily rags,
shoves them beneath the porch,
tosses the lit match.

OLDENBURG'S OBJECTS ADDRESS HIM

GEOMETRIC MOUSE

Deep in this metal head, behind my Xed-out
eyes, the mouse-sphinx knows:
small things grow tall, hard objects melt,

touch bisects every angle —
the mind's equations become a life.
You made these disc-ears, window-eyes, a door

for nose. No choice now. If I tilt
with you, talk rodent-vector talk,
the lines and points of argument are yours,

the voice is mine. Welcome to pure
fabrication, land of the Maztec ziggurat,
the matter's heart: Maus haus.

CLOTHESPIN

You've locked two halves in one —
how shall we last? Shall we embrace
in bronze or steel or stone —

or hold fast to this dream of wood:
soft pine, curled spring tipped to sun,
clipping shirt and nightgown scrubbed

to boney thread, dancing the laundry waltz.
How fine to kiss this kiss,
make Monday with our lips!

The news spins down the line:
paired legs and sleeves and sheets —
the rule of twos will keep.

TYPEWRITER ERASER

Push me—I'm a secretary,
supine, black-stockinged legs in air.
Right me—I'm a tiger at the keys.

My position's malleable:
bird, tornado, windmill, waterfall—
I roll, I fly, I twist and I've been

broccoli and octopus.
But yesterday's food for thought is today's
revolutionary. When I've turned to,

swept clean the house your ramblings built,
I'll vanish, leaving all those words
you wrote and didn't mean, indelible.

STANDING MITT WITH BALL

We don't ask much—just knuckles,
spit, and time to practice getting it
together (the sound of one hand clapping

one ball). Sometimes when the bleachers
roar, we dream our former lives:
oyster and pearl, milkweed seedpod,

mother and child of the summer world. Then
we snap back to work, to make the meeting
worth the whole quick diamond's sparkle.

As darkness falls and green clouds rise,
the filament between us glows. Now—
aim throw curve spin *thwack* and fit.

IN ART

In art you have to shoot your grandmother...
Reuben Nakian, *N.Y. Times*

"So even though she was kind of a sweet old lady,
She became, I'm sorry to say, insane.
Guns were big among my people—Brother nicked

My shins with BB's, Dad kept cleaning his 22,
Slept with a pistol inches from his head.
The winter I was 13 I shot an 'unloaded' rifle

Out the picture window & the whole thing shattered.
For years I was the picture of charity, thinking
My parents had put her away for convenience,

That if I complained, they'd do the same to me.
I hated the 3 locked doors, the ring of keys.
But so what if you're nuts, you can still make sense.

For years she wrote letters describing the squirrels
Outside her window, the iced branches, & I'd write her
About my life, my art. I think she even loved me,

At least before the lobotomy mix-mastered her brains.
After that they didn't let me visit, but she talked
More, ate more, became 'nothing but a burden,'

200 lbs of stalled flesh. They said she might as well
Go home, & she wrote a bunch of 'salad' confessions
That would have blown the family lid.

So you can see why I had to take care of her
That way. To eliminate that old defective woman
Before she came too close & gave me her disease."

III

MOVING THROUGH SEURAT
A Sunday Afternoon on the Island of La Grande Jatte

The dots   when you step back
become forms   and the forms
as you move into them
become grains of time
hundreds of tiny Sunday afternoons
whole Mondays
years that were minutes
huge seconds   arriving   leaving

Seurat!   one dot on the calendar
sailboat stuck on its twin
one dog's decision
monkey forever leashed
and in the center of the span
that child   taking
one firm white step toward you

THE ICELANDIC TWINS

This morning when a student read her poem—
"Memories, like ducks, swim in my mind,
let my mind swim in the pond"—
the others laughed.

Her eyes closed,
she blanched, gagged, fled...
Our class went on.

Then I remembered first grade—that book—
THE ICELANDIC TWINS...

Sometimes we seize metaphors
like life-preservers
or planks to throw across
the ditches of the mind.

Today I should have done just that—
eased a board over the floe
toward a pair of frozen hands
strangely like my own.

I try to catch these notions swimming through
but now they're a menagerie—
duck   frog   dog   penguin   horse—

like the collection I was god of
back in first grade,
before the Age of Metaphor,

and just before lunch
when I threw up at school
and fled home alone
across Iceland.

MONKEY CHILD

Once in a life
you're caught
sneakers clamped
to the dark edge
of a green shutter
high on a white
stucco house.

Frieda, greasy
from the kitchen
stuck out her head,
looked up, yelled
Monkey! Get down!

Ah Frieda,
how to step down
from such high purchase—
that cliff of terror
and desire—

into the human world.

EIGHT

In my deepest place
I'm not as deep as I was then—

not like the stone well
in the springhouse I'd steal into

pulled past dank walls
dodging toads and creepers

to look again and again
down at the darkshine, again

at the watery, captured
faces of children.

In that long wait
I grew fast as wisteria vine

until the April afternoon
I climbed out the attic window

glimpsed the open cellar hole
recognized my kingdom

and jumped.

STICK FIGURES

At The Hospital for Special Surgery—
"Ruptured and Crippled"
the taxi driver had called it—
in the cold dark, the night nurse
said "Roll over," gave the needles.
Every third hour I penciled
a mark—upright or diagonal—
on the endless green plaster wall.

On the other side, a Spanish girl—
spinal fusion, no cast—
came out of ether screaming and clawing.
Four people in white held her down,
yelled for more help.
Mother found a wheelchair,
rolled me out of there.

Later, for the girl's parents,
she drew stick figures
with captions in two languages,
showing NOW: beds on casters,
legs in traction, nurses wearing
pert triangular skirts,
all under the hospital pediment,

and SOON: trees, a bench by a path,
and small people
with straight legs and spines
doing ordinary things—
sitting, standing,
taking the little stick dog for a walk...
and two girls on a seesaw—
smiling, hanging on.

LEDA, RILKE, THE SWAN AND ME

Here in my angry-corner
I'm wrestling Rilke, his god who,
losing himself, becoming a swan,

becomes himself thinking about
his own marvelous feathers.
And where was Leda then?

Ruffled by interruptions,
back against two walls,
I'm crouched to snap the way

our old bitch snapped—
my parents sighed—
"Guess we'll have to put her to sleep."

Such retribution could stop you
dog-paddling to shore, or
struggling out of a high nest, or,

as, falling, the earth stops you,
or an ether cone
before you count to five.

This is the sleep you fear
they'll put you to—the winged sleep
that doesn't care

except to pluck you up
and drop you in the place
you don't come back from.

PURITAN GLASS

Young Girl in Church

The light's high and frantic
staining the glass—Sunday—
the worst day—bees in the head

Old string bean in a white gauze dress
delivers the sermon, says
there's no health in us, asks

who among us has not sinned
Her knees burn the floor
she tongues the bitter pew rail

slides the boat in
brooms in the oarlocks—
sh, It's you, sh, It's you, sh, It's you

Vision

After swimming
changing in the bedroom
I glance out—there—

beyond the slope of the porch roof
out there on the water
in gray and black and white—

an 18th century schooner
tied up at the dock
her crew unloading cargo—

Brown bodies strain
muscles throw off light
crates pile up in the sun

I look down at my skin
suddenly shamed—
the unearned salt, drying

Samaritans

Afternoons hunting raspberries—
that's not my real life...

and I'll never be at home
inside the great houses of God.

I must have made a pact once
to enter the musty libraries,

to search the mildewed pages,
to rescue the stranded words

and find places for them—
in their new families.

HOME REMEDIES

Grandma said
"Add a pinch of sugar
to the salad dressing"

Grandpa said
"Paint the wound with iodine
and expose it to the sun"
(a fine way to incur
second degree burns
I've learned)

Mother said
"If it'd been a snake
t'would've bit you"
meaning
your stupidity
pervades my airspace
like a mongoose

No wonder
I was mesmerized
and Good

There's a remedy for Good
and not just what
you might suspect

You take this mongoose
some iodine
a pinch of sugar...

FRIENDS SCHOOL

Everyone listens, or seems to.
You are, third grader, speaking,

and the words you say, count.
New words rain down and now

it's your turn to raise the shade,
to water the plants.

And now you are that plant
and where you grow means light

to drink and flower. And now
Duty and Beauty enter

hand in hand,
to join The Society of Friends,

a few of whom still say
thee... thou...

HOCKEY

I play left wing, whip down the alley,
pass to the inner. I play right inner,
stick glued to ball, flick to center

played by me. Phalanx of forwards, we
chevron rectangles—sender, receiver,
pivot & giver. I play halfback, weaver,

scrapper, backed by fullbacks—also me.
Keeping the limedust halfmoon's edge
I mind the goalie & goal that's final.

I'm the slate of slateblue tunics,
amazon pantheon hurtling to victory.
I bring water, quarter oranges, hold

the rulebook, the whistle, the timer.
I am the curve in the oblong of battle—
the swerve the wind makes
        when it takes the green field.

HOUSE

Barn red / gray shingle / fieldstone
the houses throw open their shutters—

    dance of the leaky roof
    dance of the squeaky door
    dance of the creaky porch

Once there was a child who could love only houses.

·|·

This house is glutted with smashed trees.
Let in air!   Let light!

Let me be a prowler
and follow the sun from window to window

as in the old days
before the tall ones fell, before books.

·|·

Here a river and here a wall—
                    no, the side of a house
with blue shutters—a blue-eyed house.

Yesterday the river was flowing,
last night it stopped dead,
                    a bad miracle.

·|·

Once I tore my house apart,
                    then burned it down—
poor house, I mourned for several seasons.

But one coal remained—a tiny house,

lamp at the window
                    singing like blazes.

IV

In the woods it is all right to grieve
It's all right to see the old truths,
which we usually keep packed away
in the luggage.

—Tomas Tranströmer

RETURN TO SQUID COVE

I wanted to play the banjo—
porch hammock creaking,
uncles and cousins singing—

those were the tides I learned on.

I wanted the great blue herons
for my own,
and the pond they stood in
and the saw-toothed grass.

I wanted to sleep in their nests
and call their calls
and wait on one leg in blue clay
not blinking.

Or be their food swimming silently by,
or the wind that lifted them
or the hemlocks that held them at night.

I wanted to live without being human.

But the uncles died,
cousins went to offices—

and I've come back—
a two-legged woman breathing air,

looking hard,
not blinking as dark settles
on canvas, mosquitoes
and a rusty banjo.

WHEN A VIEW SAVES YOU

you look at it hard,
hook your eyes onto blue spruce,
search moss climbing
leadgray birch.

This seeing's likely to prickle,
scanning a mackerel sky,
a forest of difficult greens.

THE BLANKET

Each summer I unpack the World War I army blankets and take one to my cabin where I try not to write about it: an ode in praise of its many outstanding qualities: durability, warmth, indifference to the bodies it has covered. This one, the color of camouflage, has no ears, yet it extracts promises from me concerning honor and history and harsh beauty, and though I fight the urge to make too much of it, the blanket rises and assumes the form of my grandfather, swaying above my paper.

SQUID COVE SEQUENCE

Telling stories, chuckling, going on—
family, guests—

as if a moment's silence
would cause the ship to go down...

The hammock squeaks on its rusty chains
and the wooden "Fatuliva" bird—
said to fly backwards
and lay square eggs—
perched high on the corner cupboard

listens for generations...

·|·

Dreaming, I pack for the summer trip,
suitcase crammed with small wool sweaters,
the hard kind.

Where are my pencil, paper?

Large people drift through—
self-involved, shadowy...

Just enough time to repack.

Out go sweaters, and that pair of
little dark deerskin slippers.

·|·

A man has absorbed the ghost of his brother
who recently died.
Eye-lines and mouth-lines draw a new face—
cheeks puff up.

He asks questions abruptly,
stands in his own space.

When you talk to him
the brother seeps into the room.

He is one bearing the weight of two.

·|·

Born under two pounds—

my father built the incubator
that kept her alive,
that we took pride in—

she'll never be quite right.

Today a buck—huge antlers—
leaped the road before my car,

                              close call...

When you begin, you don't know the ending.

·|·

59

How do the others manage...

It must happen in a hidden place

like a rock-cave the ocean enters
                                    twice a day.

When you grieve,
                you grieve for the dead and
for the living.

INDIAN PIPES

The naturalists, name-givers,
tell us *monotropa uniflora*—
of the Family Wintergreen.

But we know what they are.
Our grandfathers' ghost-pipes
poking through their spongy roof—

the old men sitting down there
rocking and smoking,
rocking and telling stories,

reminding us...

GOOSE MARSH POND

Dusk. Southerly wind. Gulls at low altitudes.
How do they land on water...

I see them through the long vee of two pines—
index and middle finger pointing up from the forest floor—
safe in their warm place.

Across the pond—a house with two chimneys.
Here every summer and never saw it before.

The gulls carve long, elegant ellipses,
as if an old figure-skater were at the control tower.

THE IMPOSTER

Normally, I wouldn't come to a place like this—
log cabin in the woods—dark outside, dark in...
I wouldn't be the one to bring in the bayberry,
the tansy and black-eyed Susans, to light the fire,
to heat up the damp bread. I wouldn't be the one
to pick mussels, clean them, steam them in wine
and herbs. Or be the one to eat them and then sit
here at the pine table in the lamplight writing
all evening. Normally, I wouldn't be writing this
but I am.

THE GLIMPSE

The first hint of it is like the last slide
of a slide show: an empty chair and the sense
that something is up. Weeks pass and then
another "slide"—a Venetian blind—or

a mirror—you can't be sure. Again you feel
as you imagine a dog feels when his ears perk up,
and like the dog who goes back to his nap,
you decide whatever it was, it's blown over.

One day you are sitting in a room where everything—
the furniture, the dog, the time of day,
the air in the room—seem perfectly ordinary.
Then a door—closed for as long as you can remember—

slides back, and you slip out to a clear sky and sea,
and when you return, you return to one who is
not quite yourself—as if you have been inside
the slide show, the one you must have been watching,

the one with images of yourself as you used to be
and images of what you will be—all at once.
And you wonder how that could have happened, and you
go over it again: *table, chair, dog, morning, air...*

·

TOUR

And that's where the sky lives—out there—
    past the window—
    not here between chair and desk.

The slow-sailing dark cloud isn't political.

No one's angry when it thunders, let's settle that.

And if you're morose on a leaden day,
    it's only you—
    a story with a head on its neck.

You could be left to die on that cloud.

But not for long.

There's always a train passing through,
    a whistle in the air,
    a band of white monkeys...

ALIVE

There you are, walking along—
part of it without even trying...

Now the general puts down his computer,
and the politician shuts his mouth,
the birds tweet and chirp
each according to his or her truth...
yes, you are in it.

You think it is always there, waiting—
if not in the textbooks
then in the trees—

but it's not so easy to get at.

It's like a secret—something shy
hiding everywhere...

and when you feel its lacy joy,
its green heart,
for a moment you can bear everything

and not be so quick to correct yourself.

THE DOORS

At certain times the inner elevator goes down
   and finds a woman so passionate
   she can't live outside a human body.
And then the starlings all take off as one
   and she begins to rise.

Up and down, up and down—she's not that simple.

Sometimes she carries a basket—
   old-fashioned wicker, a looped handle,
   filled with flames.
Or, she lies in bed after giving birth,
   her baby too close to the edge.
   Is she irresponsible?

She wants to swim in the river that flows uphill.

The doors—soft, powerful,
   open and close like sea anemones—
   scarlet, pink, silver,
and there is the urge to dive deeper,
   to listen more closely...

WEAPONRY

Staring down the two dark barrels
of a rifle, you wonder—

is history a funnel
that has finally come to this?

Dark in there.
Long tunnels that end
in more or less the same place—
the right and left lobes of the brain.

Gorgeous eyes, the tunnels say.
They say smithereens
are their idea of beauty.

And your idea?

But who's thinking—
the dark so lovely, the tunnels
so inviting...

A VICTORY

Surely in a brutal job-ridden, Puritanical, Billy Grahamized
America, poetry of pleasure, describing the six or seven lovely
things you did that day, is a victory of sorts.

—Robert Bly

For instance planting the seed called *six or seven,*
      lovely in itself, borderline, especially
considering the six or seven layers of sleep we had to throw off
      to see something like a light, six or seven
      lights strung up for a party—amber and green
like my eyes, or the six or seven raisins in your breakfast toast
      that remind me of your brown eyes
      searching mine before you left the house
and I faced the window alone, not lonely, the pattern of frost,
      one of the last frosts of the year, bringing March
and the March hare and the silver hairs of memory
      like the silver flints the ocean shoots
      to distract us from the six or seven deep
      things it is doing:
riding its green horses over the veldt on the ocean floor dodging
      thousands of sunken warships.

POETRY FROM ALICE JAMES BOOKS